Going to the Doctor

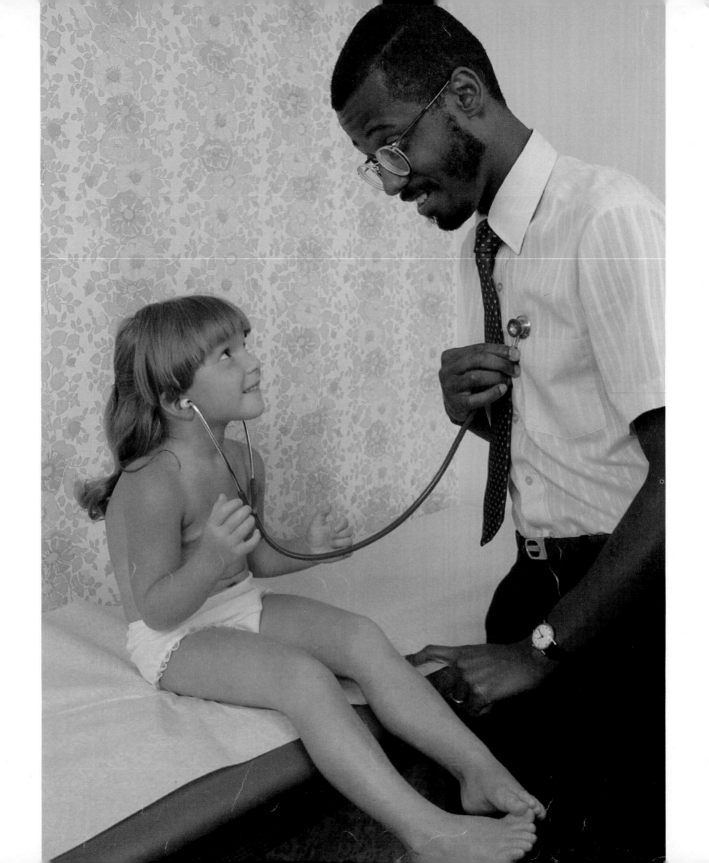

FIRST EXPERIENCES

Going to the Doctor

BY FRED ROGERS

photographs by Jim Judkis

G. P. PUTNAM'S SONS
New York

Special thanks to: Nan Earl Newell, Research; Margaret B. McFarland, Ph.D., Senior Consultant; Michael B. Rothenberg, M.D. and Mary Donnelly, M.S., Consultants; Barry N. Head; Jane Breck, M.D.; Ronald David, M.D.; the Orbison family; the Sabol family; and all of the other families and friends who helped us with the book.

Project Director: Margy Whitmer
Book design by Kathleen Westray
Library of Congress Cataloging-in-Publication Data
Rogers, Fred.   Going to the doctor.
(A Mister Rogers' first experience book)
Summary: Describes what a child can expect to see
and do on a visit to the doctor's office.
1. Children—Medical examinations—Juvenile
literature.   2. Children—Preparation for medical
care—Juvenile literature. [1. Medical care]
I. Judkis, Jim, ill.   II. Title.   III. Series:
Rogers, Fred. Mister Rogers' first experience book.
RJ50.R64   1986   616   85-24558
ISBN 0-399-21298-1
ISBN 0-399-21299-X (pbk.)
Third impression

A child's first visit with a pediatrician usually comes soon after birth. It may be months or even years later, though, that a child first shows fear about going to see a doctor.

The worry of an injection or some other unfamiliar medical procedure can trigger that fear. It can also appear because another family member may be feeling medical anxieties. And, of course, new body awareness and needs for privacy develop naturally in children's early years, so all these feelings can make it very hard for them to let doctors investigate the workings of their bodies.

Whatever the reasons, honest talk about a visit to the doctor can help lessen a child's worries. Being prepared for something that might hurt a little is easier than being surprised when it does—or wondering whether *everything* will hurt.

We can't anticipate all that will happen in a doctor's office, but we can encourage our children to voice their concerns, and we can tell them what we do know. As they learn to trust us with their questions, they can learn to trust doctors, too, as well as other important people outside the family.

Honest talk is a cornerstone of healthy trust, and with a loving, trustworthy caregiver, a child can learn to cope with many of life's new or difficult experiences.

—Fred Rogers

There are many ways parents help children
to take care of themselves. Parents show
them what's good to eat . . . and what kind
of clothes will keep them warm.

Parents show children how
to keep clean . . . and where
they can play and be safe.

Another thing parents help children understand is that doctors can help people stay healthy when they're well . . . and get better when they're sick.

Doctors know a lot about people's bodies and people's feelings. Doctors, just like all grownups, were children once. They grew up and wanted to help take care of people. Many doctors are also fathers and mothers, and they take care of their own children, too.

Doctors work in many different places. You might go to a doctor's office . . . or to a clinic . . . or even to the emergency room of a hospital.

Doctors have other people who help them with their work, too . . . people like nurses and receptionists.

They all care for many people during each day, so when you go to see the doctor, you might have to wait for your turn in a place called the *waiting room*.

Some waiting rooms have books and magazines, and some even have toys. Waiting can be hard, but if you have something to do while you're waiting, the time often seems to go faster. You might even want to bring a toy or a book from home.

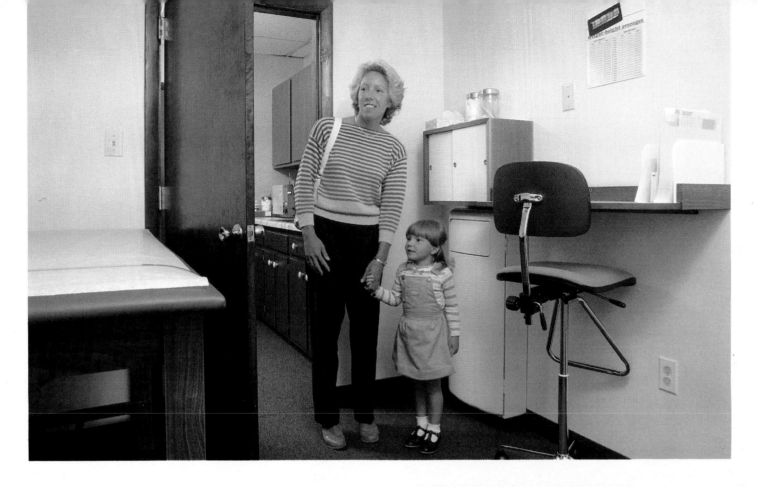

When it's your turn, you go
into the *examination room*.
The grownup who's with you
can go along, too.

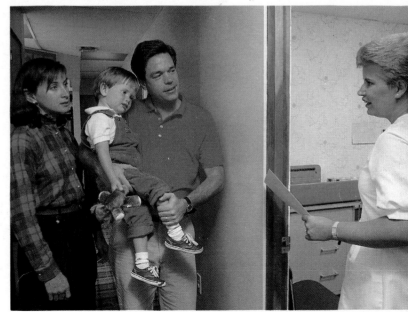

Doctors need to make sure children's bodies are healthy all over. That's why your doctor or nurse may ask you to take off your clothes. When your doctor has finished examining you, you'll be able to put all of your clothes back on again.

Doctors or nurses
measure and weigh
children. They write
down that information
each time you come
so they know how
much you've grown.

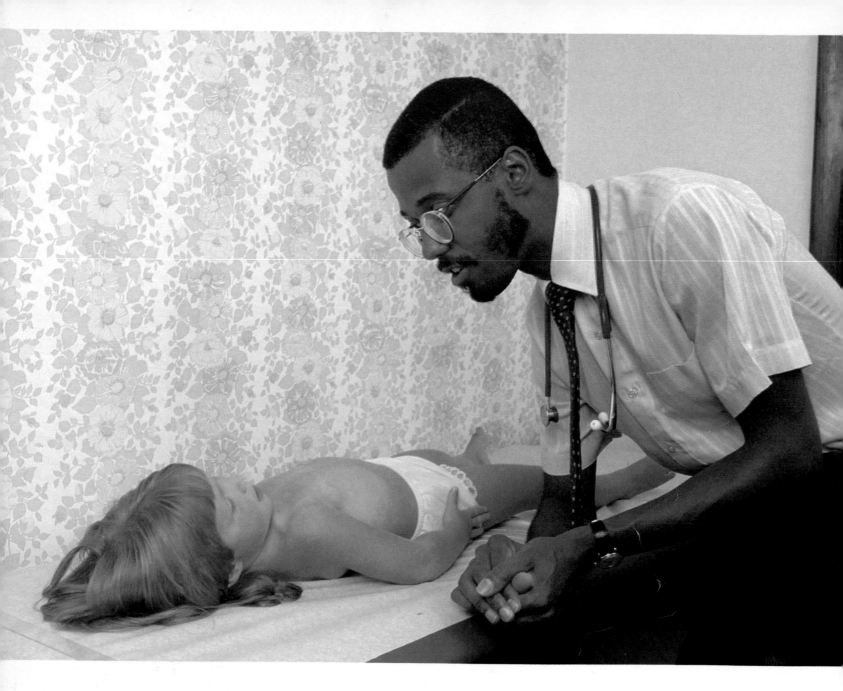

Your doctor may ask you to lie down on a
long table that has clean, white paper on it.
That's the *examination table*.

Your doctor will probably feel your stomach, your neck and under your arms. That might tickle a little bit, but the doctor is only making sure that those parts of you are healthy.

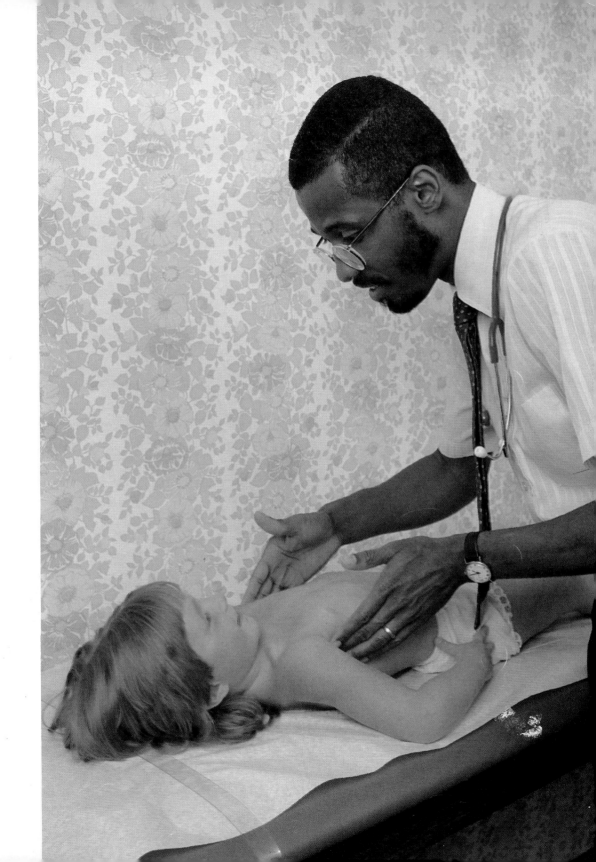

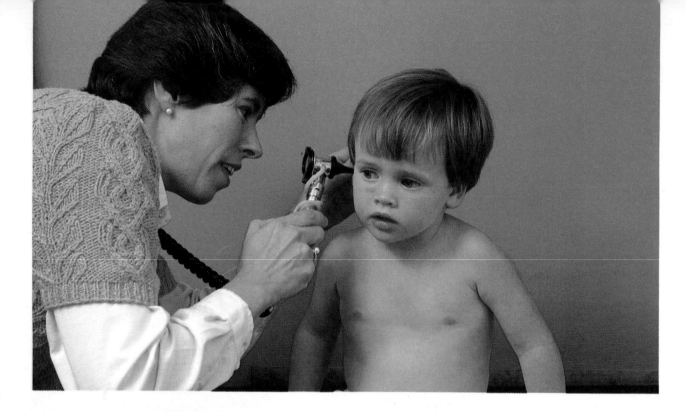

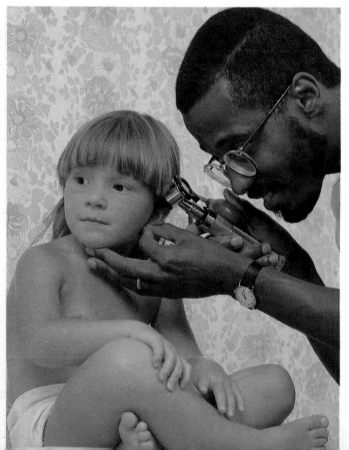

Your doctor may use
a special flashlight
called an *otoscope* to
look in your ears, your
nose, or your throat.

Your doctor may also press down on your tongue with a wooden *tongue depressor*. That makes it easier to see your throat (with the *otoscope*), but it might feel a little uncomfortable.

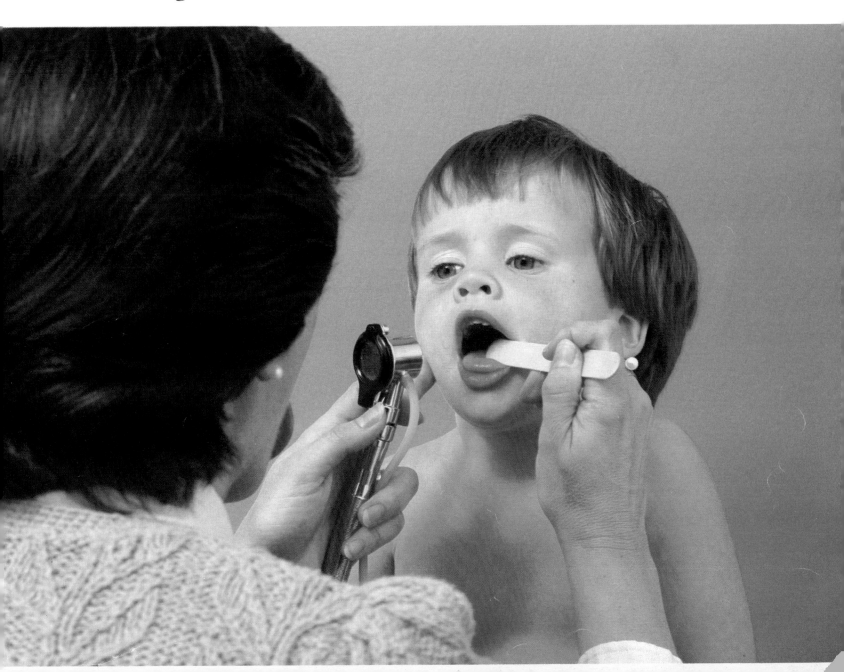

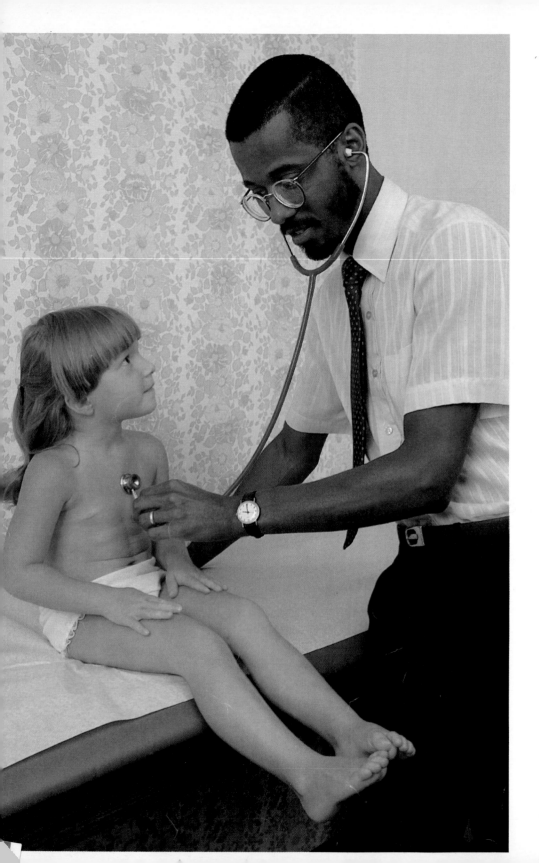

Your doctor may put a *stethoscope* on your chest to hear your heart, or on your back to hear your lungs. Your doctor may also want to listen to your stomach.

When doctors look
and listen to the
inside of your body,
they can't ever see
or hear what you're
thinking or feeling.
No one can do that!

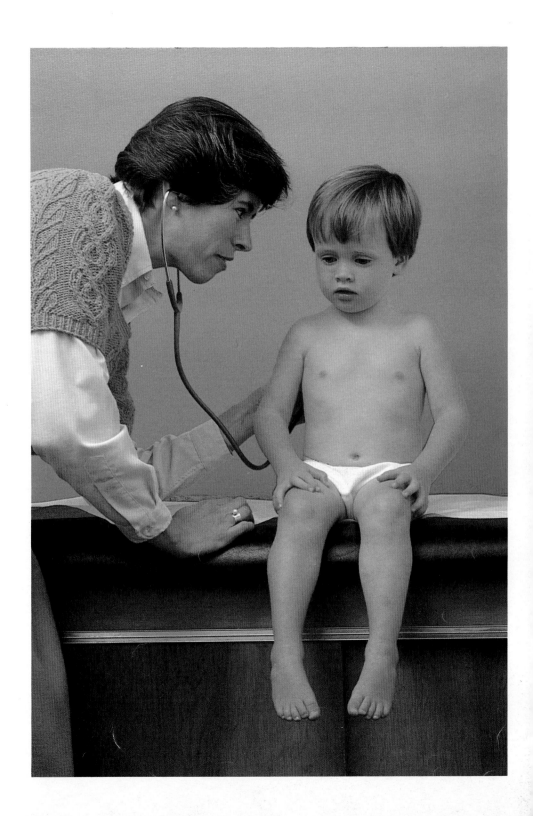

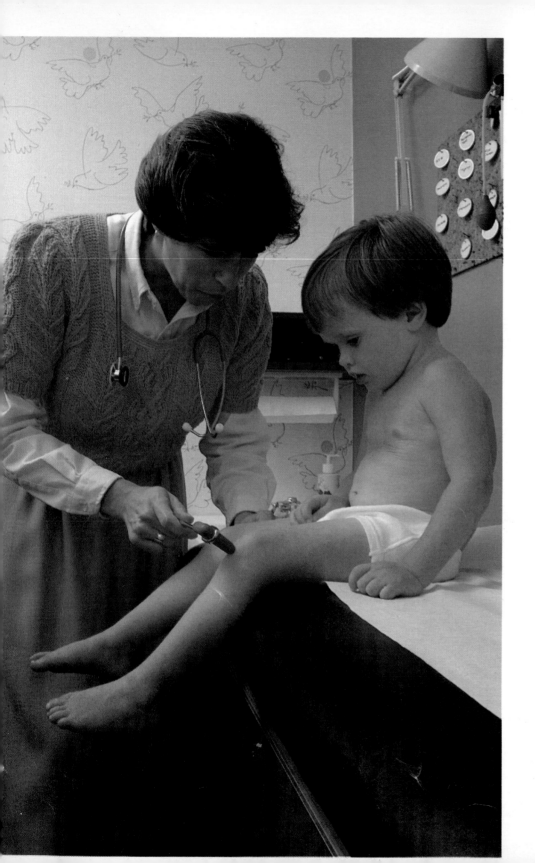

Your doctor may tap
your knee with a little
rubber hammer. That
may make your leg give
a little kick without
your even trying, but
it doesn't hurt.

All these instruments that doctors use to examine you can seem a little strange or uncomfortable, but they usually don't hurt. If you're wondering what any of these instruments do, you can ask your doctor or nurse. Your doctor might let you try out one of these instruments for yourself.

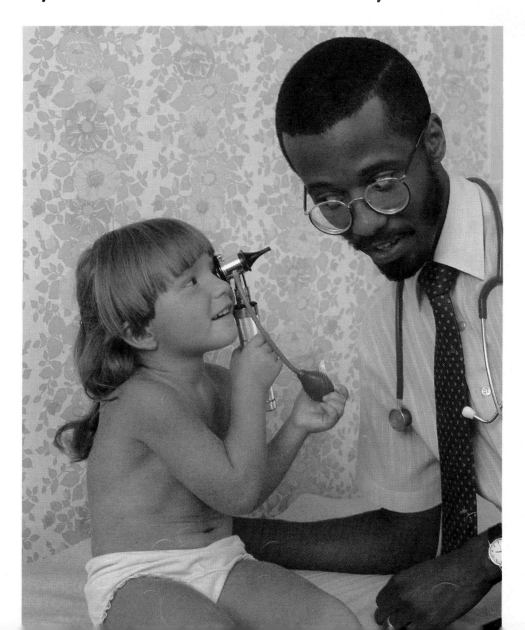

Doctors sometimes have to give their patients an *injection.* Some people call it a "shot." That *can* hurt for just a moment—like a big pinch. It might feel a little sore afterwards, too, but the hurt usually goes away very soon.

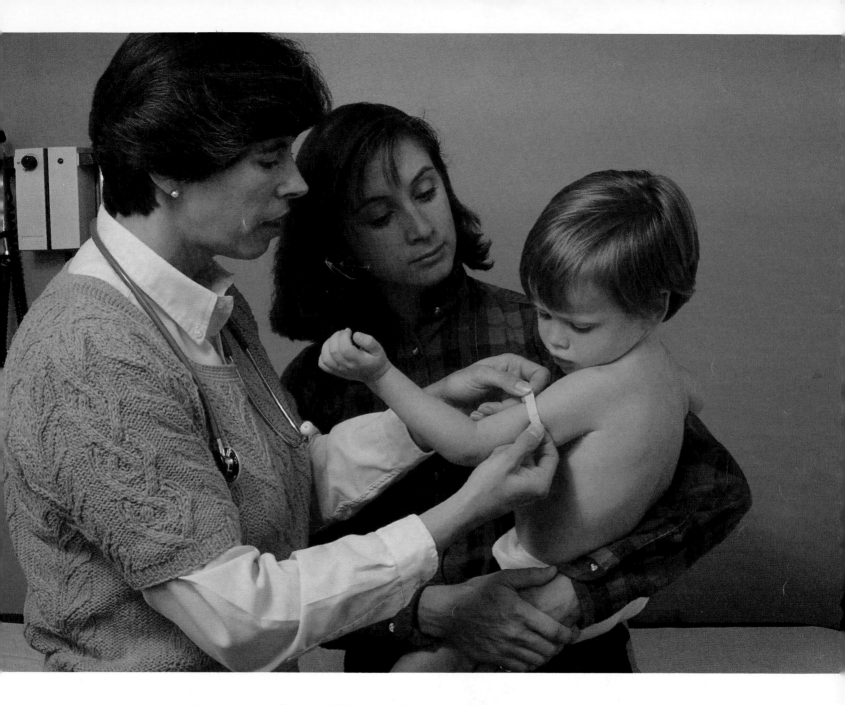

Doctors don't like to do anything to hurt
people, but they know that the quick "pinch"
of an injection is better than feeling sick for
a long time.

If you have any questions about what the doctor is doing to help you have a healthy body, it's fine to ask. Doctors know that children wonder about lots of things. Many doctors really like to hear children's questions.

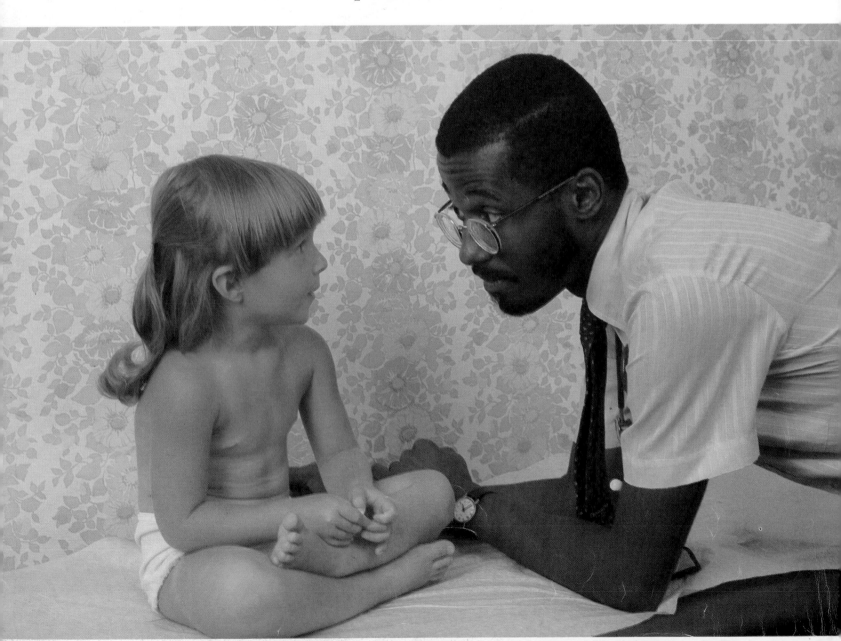

After your time with
the doctor is over, you
can get dressed and
get ready to leave.

Before you go home, your doctor may want to talk with you and your mom or dad about how to help you stay healthy, or if you're sick, how to help you get well again.

You may want to talk with the people you love about going to the doctor—and you may want to pretend about being a doctor yourself.

Taking good care of your body helps your body to grow. Talking and playing about something you wonder about helps you to grow, too. You can feel proud of the way you're growing—outside and in!